Meditations to Make You
SMILE

MARTHA J. BECKMAN
Illustrated by

John McPherson

DIMENSIONS
FOR LIVING

NASHVILLE

MEDITATIONS TO MAKE YOU SMILE

This book is printed on acid-free, recycled paper.

Library of Congress Cataloging-in-Publication Data
Beckman, Martha J., d. 1993.
    Meditations to make you smile / Martha J. Beckman.
        p. cm.
    ISBN 0-687-00781-X (pbk. : alk. paper)
    1. Meditations. I. Title.
BV4832.2.B37 1995
242—dc20   94-30674
                                                                            CIP

Except where noted Scripture quotations are from the New Revised Stand-
ard Version of the Bible, copyright © 1989 by the Division of Christian
Education of the National Council of the Churches of Christ in the USA.
Used by permission.

Those noted NIV are taken from the Holy Bible: New International Ver-
sion®. Copyright © 1973, 1978, 1984 by the International Bible Society.
Used by permission of Zondervan Publishing House.

Those noted KJV are from the King James Version of the Bible.

95 96 97 98 99 00 01 02 03 04—10 9 8 7 6 5 4 3 2 1

MANUFACTURED IN THE UNITED STATES OF AMERICA

Meditations to Make You Smile

Editor's Note

Someone has said that those whose lives are filled with laughter are the richest persons in the world. If this is true, then Martha J. Beckman was a wealthy woman indeed.

Marti Beckman was a freelance writer whose humorous and inspirational writings appeared regularly in *Mature Years* magazine and many other periodicals. Prior to her death in November 1993, Marti submitted the material for this book, which was to be her first. It is to her loving memory that this book is dedicated.

Foreword

Some days are naturally filled with sunshine and laughter, while other days seem a month long and linger like a stalled low-pressure system. How encouraging it is to have a fresh breeze and glimmers of light move across our path again. That is how I see this delightful devotional—as a refreshing way to inject lightness into our day.

Martha's succinct format allows me to fit these tickling tidbits into my busy routine while giving me direction for my attitude and a reminder of the only One who can see me through the dailiness of my existence.

As I read I smiled, I chuckled, and I laughed out loud. Martha makes her point simply and definitely. *Meditations to Make You Smile* will brighten your day as well as your countenance.

Patsy Clairmont
Author of *God Uses Cracked Pots*

Meditations to
Make You Smile

A grandmother asked her grand-daughter what her favorite vegetable was. She replied, "Punkins."

"Why pumpkins?" the grandmother asked.

"Because they smile a lot!"

Think about your favorite people. They probably are people who smile a lot, and they probably are people who make you smile a lot, too! If your friends and family were asked to list those people who make them smile, would your name be on the list?

You give us so much to smile about, God, yet sometimes I still don't feel like smiling. At those times, fill me with your transforming love.

11

A mother tucked her daughter into bed. As she left her, she looked out the hall window to see white flakes swirling and said, without thinking, "Lord, look at it snow!"

A sleepy voice responded, "You don't have to tell him, Mommy; he already knows."

What a comforting thought! The Lord knows what we are thinking and is looking out for us, even as we perceive trouble. He never will give us a burden too heavy to carry but will help us carry the load. And, at times of terrible anguish, he will be ready to carry us. Our faith will let us rest peacefully in his gentle arms.

Thank you, Lord, for keeping me in your constant care.

Two weeks after seven-year-old John had his tonsils removed, his mother received the bill. She commented on how high the bill was. John was even more astonished than his mother. He said, "You mean I had to go through all that, and we have to pay for it, too?"

If we had only one temporary affliction to bear in our lifetime, then life would be grand for everyone! Who could not bear up under a temporary illness or injury? But often insult is added to injury. We all experience loss and grief as long as we live. Our lives must be lived out in divine perspective, for many of us, our families, and our friends have much to bear.

O eternal God, keep before me that "this slight momentary affliction is preparing us for an eternal weight of glory beyond all measure" (2 Cor. 4:17).

A teacher asked her students to think of a Bible story and draw a picture of it. One child handed in a drawing of a long limousine with three faces peering from it. The teacher asked her what the drawing portrayed.

"That's God, driving Adam and Eve out of the Garden of Eden."

What a delightful image: God journeyed with Adam and Eve when they left the garden. They were not alone. God not only went with them; God was in the driver's seat. How good it is to know that God is always in the driver's seat!

God, I am so grateful that you guide and direct me each and every day. With you in the driver's seat of my life, there is nothing I should fear.

A hesitant driver, waiting for a traffic jam to clear, came to a complete stop on the freeway ramp. The traffic thinned, but the driver still waited.

Finally a furious voice from the vehicle behind him cried, "The sign says 'Yield,' not give up!"

Like the hesitant driver, we sometimes lose all hope of making it through the traffic jams of our own daily lives. We throw our hands up in despair and cry, "Why, Lord?" Although sometimes we do have to yield to the unavoidable circumstances of life, we never have to give up hope. Jesus said that all things are possible to those who have faith, even the faith of a tiny mustard seed.

Lord, it's easy to have faith when all is well. Strengthen my faith when the difficult days come.

Two women on a bus were discussing the play one of them had seen the night before. "Did it have a happy ending?" one woman asked of her friend who had attended the play. Her friend replied, "Yeah, everyone was happy when it ended!"

Anticipation that ends in disappointment is common to us all. Things don't always turn out as we expect. Although our lives and our labors may not always come to happy endings, God promises us an abundant life with an eternal ending! And that can be had only by trusting God completely in spite of all our disappointments.

O God of every ending and beginning, remind me daily that "we walk by faith, not by sight" (2 Cor. 5:7).

Two elderly friends were chatting. One said, "You know, people our age are already living in the hereafter."

"What do you mean?" her friend replied.

"Well, I find myself walking into any part of the house and immediately asking myself, 'What did I come here after?' "

In a sense, we really are living in the "hereafter." God's kingdom is both here and hereafter. Jesus spoke of the Kingdom "in your midst" and the Kingdom "yet to come." The gift of eternal life abides in us now, but it also is something yet to come. The Kingdom is a way of life as well as a life to come.

O God, help me to remember that your kingdom is both here and hereafter.

After putting her children to bed, a mother changed into old slacks and a droopy blouse and proceeded to wash her hair. As she heard the children getting more and more rambunctious, her patience grew thin. At last she threw a towel around her head and stormed into their room, putting them back to bed with stern warnings. As she left the room, she heard her three-year-old say with a trembling voice, "Who was that?"

We all have a side of ourselves that we rarely reveal. We can never be fully known except by the One who made us. With God, we can strive to be completely honest, for we are already known in judgment, in understanding, and above all, in love!

O loving God, I rejoice that you made us, keep us, and will never let us go!

21

A mother carefully poured out six glasses of one-calorie-per-bottle soda as her son watched. When she was finished, he said, "I wonder who got the calorie?"

The scope of God's love is unfathomable to us. We can grasp it only on a very small scale—loving a second child as much as the first; finding room in our crowded lives for a new and cherished friend; making a difference in someone else's life. But in such glimpses we come to know God a bit better, and we are so grateful for that.

Dear God, my love for you does not begin to reflect your love for me. Help me catch glimpses of your everlasting love.

My grandson was telling me that he and his three playmates attended different churches. Then he added, "It really doesn't matter if we go to different churches, does it, Grandma, as long as we're all Republicans?"

God cares not what political party we support nor what church we attend. What matters to God is what is in our hearts and minds and how we live our lives. Today let us live joyfully in God's love!

Today and every day, I praise you, Lord, for your unconditional love.

With a critical eye, my granddaughter watched as I ladled ice cream into her dish. Since the amount I usually gave her never seemed to be enough, I asked her, "How much would you like?"

She thought it over and then said, judiciously, "Give me too much!"

God is ready, willing, and able to give each of us "too much." Everything we have has been given to us by God, our loving Father. How lucky we are! How blessed! God knows our needs and showers us with his abundance!

Praise God from whom all blessings flow.

Two little boys were visiting their grandfather, and he took them to a restaurant for lunch. They couldn't make up their minds about what they wanted to eat. Finally the grandfather grinned at the server and said, "Just bring them bread and water."

One of the little boys looked up and quavered, "Can I have ketchup on it?"

God gives us the freedom to make decisions for ourselves. Like this small boy, we sometimes have difficulty deciding. Then God, like this grandfather, will choose for us. Even in our failure to act, we may criticize another trying to help us. Still, we can expect God's good gifts.

God, I try to be responsible but sometimes fail. Help me in those times to see your gifts and to be grateful.

A young man was taking a verbal test to join the local police force. The questioner asked, "If you were driving a police car, alone on a lonely road at night, and were being chased by a gang of criminals driving sixty miles an hour, what would you do?"

The young man answered without a second's thought: "Seventy!"

No matter how fast we may run from our problems, they have a way of catching up to us. Though we are quick to ask for God's help, we hesitate to give up our control. But true peace comes when we turn the problem over to God's care and then trust God to see us through. No problem is ever too great for God!

God, help me to let go and trust you.

Little John was five years old and was attending Bible school. The children in his class were to memorize the Lord's Prayer, and he was trying diligently. One afternoon as he was sitting on his bedroom floor, head bowed, his mother heard him reverently say, "Our Father, who art in Heaven, how did you know my name?"

How does God know our names? As difficult as it is to comprehend, our God is an all-knowing, all-seeing God. The Bible tells us God sees even a sparrow's fall. We can be assured that he sees our every move and mood. He laughs when we laugh and cries when we cry. He is our soul's delight and succor. We are important to him, each one of us.

Dear God, I know you know my inmost thoughts, for you have chosen me for your own. I trust your love and care.

A group of school children visited the local police station and viewed the pictures of the ten most wanted criminals. One child pointed to a picture and asked if it was really a picture of a wanted person.

"Yes," answered the guide.

"Well, then," said the child, "why didn't you keep him when you took his picture?"

In a manner of speaking, we all are "wanted" persons—wanted not for punishment but for inclusion in the family of God. To share in the joy of the family, all we have to do is stop running and go "home."

The very thought of you, Lord, fills my heart with gladness. How grateful I am to be part of your family.

As Josie went up to bed, her mother reminded her to say her prayers. The next morning, she asked Josie if she had prayed.

Josie answered, "Well, I started to, but then I thought that God must get awfully tired of hearing the same things, so I crawled into bed and told him the story of the three bears."

Does God ever get tired of hearing our prayers? No more so than a small child is likely to get tired of hearing the story of the three bears. When we pray with the faith and joy of children, we, like them, can feel the gaiety of God's love and rest secure in the knowledge that God is always eager to listen.

Gracious Father, help me to pray with the unwavering faith and joyful spirit of a child.

The rains ended, and Noah told the animals to go forth and multiply. All the animals obeyed, except for two snakes who were hiding in a corner.

"Didn't you hear me say to go forth and multiply?" Noah asked them.

They looked up at him woefully and replied, "We can't; we're adders!"

Sometimes our lives get so demanding and hectic that we can't focus on what others are saying to us. We probably seem a little dense! And if we are having trouble communicating with our own families and friends, we might find it especially difficult to hear God's voice.

Dear God, let me appreciate the gift of silence. Be with me as I try to take time each day to listen to what you are saying to me.

A doctor apologized for keeping an elderly woman waiting so long in his office.

"That's all right," she said demurely. "I just thought you'd like to treat my illness while it was in its early stages!"

Sometimes it's difficult to have patience. But when we lose our patience, we often also lose our temper and say or do something that we later regret. The Gospel of Luke says that those with an honest and good heart keep the word of God and "bring forth fruit with patience" (8:15 KJV). And the book of James reminds us to "let patience [work] her perfect work" (1:4 KJV) so that we may become mature and complete persons. It is when we live with patience and faithfulness that we discover true peace.

Lord, have patience with me as I strive to be a more patient person.

I walked into my six-year-old grandson's room to kiss him good-night and found it with wall-to-wall toys, books, and clothing. I asked him, "How can you live in such a mess?"

He smiled knowingly and said, "I step like the song we sang in Sunday school this morning: 'Softly and Tenderly.' "

How do we step into people's lives, "softly and tenderly" or carrying big sticks? How often are we on the defensive, looking at others through eyes of suspicion, irritation, or even hate?

Jesus taught us that we are to love one another. When we allow love to rule our lives and relationships, it becomes second nature to interact with others with gentleness and joy.

Dear Loving God, help me to make love the center of my life.

An automobile transport trucker's headlights went out. So he stopped on the side of the road, climbed onto the trailer, turned on the lights of the front car, returned to the cab of the truck, and continued driving. A few miles down the road, an approaching car swerved suddenly and ran off the road into a ditch.

The trucker pulled off the road, stopped, and went over to the car to see if he could help. "Why did you swerve off the road?" he asked the car's driver.

The driver replied, "Well, I figured that if you were as wide as you were tall, I'd never get past you!"

Things are not always what they seem! We learn this lesson again and again, yet we are so easily deceived. Outside appearances and first impressions cloud our vision; comments taken out of context lead to false assumptions and conclusions; misguided perceptions elicit hasty decisions. We need to remember to look at situations and people more slowly, more carefully, and more completely—to look for the truth and beauty within.

Help me to see things as they really are, Lord, and to find the beauty and goodness within others.

A Bible school teacher asked her students to write letters to God, thanking him for his many blessings. One child wrote, "Dear Heavenly Father, thank you for my parents, my grandparents, and my sister, Angie. I apologize for my brother, Davy. I don't think you're through working on him yet. Sincerely, Phil."

Isn't it wonderful that God is never through working on us, no matter how long we live? We can always improve. If we are sorry for our sin and ask God for forgiveness, we are given a fresh start. Each day really is a new beginning, ripe with possibilities.

Dear God, thank you for this new day and the opportunities it brings.

A little boy was roughhousing with his dog. His mother said to him, "Now, Peter, I know you love Granger, but you're loving him too much. How would you feel if someone huge picked you up and squeezed you so hard you couldn't breathe?"

The boy thought a moment and then said, "I guess I'd feel like it was my birthday and Aunt Doreen was here!"

We all know people who love "too much"—their demonstrations of love are suffocating, manipulative, or perhaps even exploitative. The love Christ demonstrated and the love we are called to give is selfless love—love that places the needs and well-being of others above self.

Lord, help me to follow your perfect example of selfless love.

Whenasked what she wanted for her birthday, little Sarah said, "One of everything, please!"

Many of us never outgrow the selfishness of our early childhood years. We, too, want "one of everything, please." It seems that the more we accumulate, the longer our lists of wants and "needs" become. In our consumer-driven society, it's difficult to break out of this cycle of self-gratification.

Yet we know from Christ's example that we are to be more concerned about the needs of others than our own. We are to look for ways to help others rather than ways to help ourselves. And in helping others we discover something amazing: When we give to others we receive more joy and gratification than material things could ever bring us.

Lord, forgive me for thinking of myself first. Transform my selfish desires into genuine concern for the needs of others.

A new neighbor asked the little girl next door if she had any brothers and sisters. She replied, "No, I'm the lonely child."

Are you a lonely child? There is no need for loneliness when you follow Jesus' instruction to seek out other "lonely children" and meet their needs. As we reach out to others in love, we find that our hearts also are filled.

Lord, help me to think of others who are lonelier than I am. Use me to help bring them happiness, and thus improve my life as well.

A mother took her three-year-old daughter to church for the first time just before Easter. The church lights were lowered, and then the choir came down the aisle, carrying lighted candles. All was quiet until the little one started to sing in a loud voice, "Happy birthday to you, happy birthday to you . . ."

We have much to learn from the spontaneous outpourings of children's celebratory spirits and joyful hearts. When the disciples tried to keep the children from Jesus, he said to them: "Let the little children come to me; do not stop them; for it is to such as these that the kingdom of God belongs" (Mark 10:14b).

Loving Father, give me the heart of a child.

A mother was telling her little girl what her own childhood was like: "We used to skate outside on a pond. I had a swing made from a tire; it hung from a big tree in our front yard. We rode our pony, Lindbergh. We picked wild raspberries in the woods."

The little girl was wide-eyed, taking this in. At last she said, "I sure wish I'd gotten to know you sooner!"

We are fortunate if we have grown up in the church, learning of the love of God as children. But many children are not so fortunate. The good news is that we may reach out to them and teach them of God's life-changing love.

What can you do to help a child "get to know God"?

Dear God, help me be an instrument of your love.

A boy said to his father after a homework session, "It's okay for you to say math is easy. You figure in your head—I have to use a computer!"

What is easy for one to accomplish may be quite difficult for another. And when one fails to understand and accept another's capabilities and limits, hurt feelings and anger can follow. Empathy, an honest attempt to put yourself in the place of another, will keep or restore good cheer.

Thank you, God, for always understanding me and accepting me. Help me to be more like you every day.

Sir," said the timid employee to his boss, "my wife says I'm to ask you for a raise."

"Fine," the boss replied. "I'll ask my wife if I can give you one."

Prayer is conversation with God. Sometime when you hesitate to ask for something in prayer, simply talk with God about your concern. Then listen. Then you might want to talk some more. Then listen again. Continuing dialogue with God is a fitting habit for a Christian.

Dear God, let me hear you in the stillness. When I call, answer me.

A patient complained to his psychiatrist, "Doctor, everyone calls me a liar."

"Oh, come now," the doctor replied. "I don't believe that!"

Like the well-intentioned doctor, sometimes we try to "be nice" or make others feel good about themselves when we should be lovingly honest. Too often we seek the approval of others rather than the approval of God. As Christians, we are called to hold one another accountable as well as to encourage one another in the faith.

Dear God, help me always to seek your approval in all things.

A woman took her Social Security check to the bank to cash it. Although the check was plainly marked "Do not fold, staple, or mutilate," she had rumpled it considerably. The teller told her, "You should be more careful with your checks. The government doesn't like it when you muss them up."

The woman replied, "Well then, we're even. I don't like some of the things the government does, either!"

Although we are generally not as vocal about our dislike of God's requirements as we are about the requirements of the government, most of us, at one time or another, have been confused, upset, or even angered by something that God has asked of us. It's not always easy to do God's will. And sometimes when we try our very best to do what God would have us do, we are met with nothing but frustration, condemnation, or even aggression.

Though we may be tempted to give up or give in, Christ reminds us that God's will is perfect and there is nothing that cannot be accomplished by those who place their trust in him. May we follow Christ's example as we strive to do God's will.

Dear God, strengthen me with resolve, courage, and faith so that I may do your will day by day.

My young grandson was visiting one day when he asked, "Grandma, do you know how you and God are alike?"

I mentally polished my halo while I asked, "No, how are we alike?"

"You're both old," he replied.

God was, is, and always shall be. God is eternal, constant. No matter how the world may change, God remains constant. No matter how our lives may change, God remains constant. In a day of increasing change, it is reassuring to know that we are guided by a constant, never-changing God.

Eternal God, I know you are with me always. Give me direction as I face exciting and unsettling changes in my life and my world.

A little girl was diligently pounding away on her father's typewriter. She told him she was writing a story.

"What's it about?" he asked.

"I don't know," she replied. "I can't read."

Many of our pioneer ancestors learned to read by using the Bible—often the only book they had. Today we have our own libraries full of books, but "the good book" is still the best reading for our souls, our minds, and our lives.

Dear Gracious Master, help me use my ability to read your Word to further your work in the world. Let me introduce others to your Word and thus help to give them joyful hearts.

I didn't know if my granddaughter had learned her colors yet, so I decided to test her. I would point out something and ask what color it was. She would tell me, and always she was correct. But it was fun for me, so I continued. At last she headed for the door, saying sagely, "Grandma, I think you should try to figure out some of these yourself!"

Just as we often test children, so also God tests us constantly to help us grow—and is delighted when we do right. God likes to see us think for ourselves, using our knowledge of his Word as our guide.

Dear God, thank you for the Bible, which teaches our minds and hearts how you want us to live.

AND HOW ABOUT THIS BALL, JULIE?! WHAT COLOR IS IT?!
OH, BROTHER! WHEN IS SHE GOING TO LEARN HER COLORS?!
McPherson

A little girl overheard her mother complaining about her varicose veins to a neighbor. Later, when the girl's mother didn't go to the annual school play, the teacher asked why. The little girl answered, "My mother has very close veins, and they're bothering her."

Often we are like little children in our approach to God's Word. We truly believe we understand God's message, yet our understandings are no more than our personal interpretations of God's meaning. To understand God's Word we must do more than read the Scripture; we must meditate upon it, study it, discuss it, and pray for understanding, all the while opening our minds and hearts to God's still, small voice.

Instill the meaning of your Word upon my heart, O God.

A man was driving a sports car down highway 89 at 90 miles an hour. A highway patrol officer stopped him and asked, "Didn't you see the speed limit sign back there?"

"Yes, sir, I did. It said eighty-nine miles per hour."

The officer sighed and said, "Oh, brother. I'm glad I caught you before you got to Route 251!"

We often travel through life like the man in the sports car, making careless judgments as we speed from one activity to the next. When we make an effort to slow down and give each area of our lives the attention it deserves, asking for God's guidance and wisdom, we reap the benefits of a richer, more joyful life.

Slow me down, Lord, and give me the wisdom to make good decisions.

Allen was promised a new puppy for his tenth birthday. He had a hard time deciding on the puppy he wanted. Finally he chose the most nondescript one in the lot, but one whose tail had never stopped wagging all the time he'd been there. When asked why he chose that puppy, he replied, "I want the one with the happy ending."

We all want happy endings—in our TV shows, our books, our sports, and our lives. Although we will not always have happy endings in this life, Jesus promises us the happiest ending of all: eternal life in the kingdom of God. When we have faith in this promise, we have hope for the living of every day of this life.

Dear Lord, I am grateful for the hope you have given me with your promise of eternal life.

A ten-year-old, under the tutelage of her grandmother, was becoming quite knowledgeable about the Bible. Then one day she floored her grandmother by asking, "Which Virgin was the mother of Jesus: the Virgin Mary or the King James Virgin?"

Our diligent efforts to increase our knowledge or skills do not save us from making embarrassing blunders. Yet despite how others may react to those mistakes, we must not become discouraged. The pursuit of knowledge is honorable and worthy of our efforts. As Solomon reminds us, "An intelligent mind acquires knowledge, and the ear of the wise seeks knowledge" (Prov. 18:15).

Dear God, enable me to become all that you have created me to be.

A Sunday school class was studying the Ten Commandments. They were ready to discuss the last one. The teacher asked if anyone could tell her what it was.

Susie raised her hand, stood tall, and quoted, "Thou shalt not take the covers off thy neighbor's wife."

Sometimes we don't get the words just right, but we do get the message. Coveting often leads to uncovering. God wants to communicate with us and uses all of our faculties to do it. In this day of permissiveness and garbled communications, we can still know God's commandments. And we can still obey.

Father, I certainly don't have everything figured out. But I do know that there is still right and there is still wrong. I know that I can choose between them. Thank you for holding me accountable.

A man went to see the doctor because his eyes had popped out of their sockets and his ears were ringing. The doctor's diagnosis was that the man needed to have his tonsils removed. That was done, but his condition did not improve. A second doctor told him that he needed to have his teeth pulled. That was done, but his condition remained the same. A third doctor proclaimed that the man had only six months to live.

So the man decided to live it up. He bought a sports car, hired a chauffeur, and had the best tailor in town make him three new suits and five new shirts. As the tailor was measuring him for the apparel, he recited, "A 34 sleeve, a 16 collar . . ."

"Wait a minute," the man interrupted. "I've always worn a 15 collar."

"No, 16 collar," the tailor said as he measured again.

"No, only a 15!" the man argued.

"Listen," the tailor said. "Keep on wearing a 15 collar and your eyes will pop out and your ears will ring!"

Solomon said it well: "The wise lay up knowledge, but the babbling of a fool brings ruin near" (Prov. 10:14).

Dear God, as I grow in knowledge may I also grow in wisdom.

A little girl was reciting in class: "Courtesy is to do something good, while politeness is not to do something bad. The best way to help your parents is to act behavingly."

God calls us to act "behavingly," and this involves much more than being courteous or polite. It involves doing the right and loving thing, sometimes despite unpleasant consequences. It involves loving neighbor as self. It involves servanthood and sacrifice. It involves nothing less than being a disciple of Jesus Christ.

Dear Lord, help me to be a faithful disciple day by day.

A very dirty little fellow came in from playing in the yard and asked his mother, "Who am I?"

Ready to play the game, she said, "I don't know! Who are you?"

"Wow!" cried the child. "Mrs. Johnson was right! She said I was so dirty, my own mother wouldn't recognize me!"

Sometimes our guilt makes us feel so dirty that we hope God will not recognize us. But no matter how "dirty" we may become, God loves us and forgives us. If we are sorry for our sin and ask for God's forgiveness, God will bring peace to our minds and souls.

Thank you, God, for your forgiving, never-ending love.

A teacher was sitting at her desk grading papers when her first-grade class came back from lunch. Alice informed the teacher, "Paul has to go to the principal's office."

"I wonder why?" the teacher mused.

"Because he's a following person," Alice replied.

"A what?" the teacher asked.

"It came over the loudspeaker: 'The following persons are to go to the office.'"

Alice put her own interpretation on the phrase "following person." But think about it. We truly are "following persons" if we have taken seriously Jesus' invitation, "Follow me."

Dear God, help me to follow Jesus.

Five-year-old Jane was late for school. Her kindergarten teacher met her at the classroom door and said, "Good morning, Jane. I was beginning to worry about you. Why are you late?"

Jane handed her teacher a geranium and said, "Sometimes I just have to wait until they bloom."

Waiting is difficult for us, whether we are waiting for our flowers to bloom or for a child who is inexplicably late. Patience is a virtue we seldom consider unless we really need it; and then it is least likely to come easily. If you know anyone who seems to have the gift of patience, ask that person for one hint that might help you.

Dear God, how patient you are with me! Be with me as I try to make things a little easier for you.

Little Ricky opened the large family Bible and gazed in awe at a dried, pressed leaf. "Look," he said in a hushed voice, "Adam's suit!"

Adam and Eve were naked in the Garden and felt no need to cover themselves until they had their sin to hide. But they couldn't hide their sin from God.

We, too, try to hide our sin, but God sees all and mourns our actions. Still, God longs to forgive us. When we seek his forgiveness, we are clothed in his love.

Dear God, forgive me for trying to hide my sin.

A customer in a pet store was going from cage to cage looking for a parakeet that could talk. As she stopped at each cage, she said to the parakeet inside, "If you can talk, say something." Each time the parakeet stared at her in silence.

Finally, at the last cage, the parakeet replied, "Yeah, I can talk. Can you fly?"

How often have we treated people the same way this customer treated the parakeet? We expect so much of another while asking so little of ourselves. Fortunately for us, God intends to give much more than he receives. We would find it impossible to match God's grace.

Dear God, thank you that your great expectations of us are surpassed by your expectations of yourself. That makes me want to try harder to be the best person I can be.

A couple bought a new car. Several weeks later, the wife scratched the side of the car as she backed it out of the garage. When she told her husband about it, tears rolled down her cheeks. He hugged and consoled her, saying, "That's all right. Just take it to the garage and have it fixed."

A week later, she backed the car into a pole and broke a taillight. Again she cried as she told her husband about it, and again he hugged her and said, "That's all right. Just bad luck. Take it to the garage and have it fixed."

"But I'm embarrassed to take it back so soon," she said.

He shrugged and said with a smile, "If you're embarrassed, tell them I did it."

She wailed, "That's what I told them the first time!"

We have been blaming others and making excuses for our sin ever since that tragic episode with the apple in the Garden. When God confronted Adam, he blamed Eve; and when God confronted Eve, she blamed the serpent. And so it has gone through the ages.

Admitting our sin is never easy, but it is the first step in our repentance. Our inability to confess that we have done wrong separates us from God's grace. When we open our hearts to God, acknowledging our need for his forgiveness, we are made whole again.

Gracious God, help me to recognize and admit my sin rather than blame others. I stand in need of your forgiving love.

The teacher asked Johnny, "Where is Brazil?"

Johnny stalled a moment and then said, "Where do you think it is?"

The teacher replied, "I don't think; I know."

Johnny grinned and said, "I don't think I know, either!"

Often we're like Johnny; we knowingly misinterpret what others say or do to suit our needs. Sometimes, we rationalize, it's more convenient to apologize after the fact. Perhaps we forget or even deny that God knows our dishonesty, even when others do not. When we are honest with ourselves and with God, it is easier to be honest with others.

God, help me to be more honest.

After searching for a parking space for some time, an exasperated man finally parked in a "no parking" zone. He left this message on his car: "I've circled this block ten times, and I couldn't find a place to park. I have an urgent appointment and must keep it or lose my job. Forgive us our trespasses."

When he returned to his car, he found this note: "I've circled this block for ten years. If I don't give you a ticket, I'll lose my job. Lead us not into temptation."

Often we try to justify our actions by making excuses—all the while knowing that what we are doing is wrong. Our motto is "Ask for forgiveness, not permission." Others may not know our hearts, but God does. God knows when we are sincere and when we are bluffing. To receive God's forgiveness, we must admit our sin and be genuinely sorry for what we have done. Then God's grace flows freely and abundantly!

Dear God, help me to resist the temptation to make excuses for my sin. I stand in need of your abundant and amazing grace.

Little Darlene surprised her mother with this postscript to her bedtime prayer: "And, Dear Lord, please send the beautiful snow to keep the flowers warm through the winter." Then she climbed into bed and said to her mother, "That time I fooled God. I want the snow so I can go sliding on my new sled!"

Sometimes we try to fool God, but God knows what's in our minds and hearts. God knows us better than we know ourselves and, despite our failings, loves us still. Isn't it liberating to realize that we can be nothing but our true selves before God!

Dear All-knowing God, help me always to come before you in honesty.

The mechanic looked the old car over carefully and then rendered this verdict: "Keep the oil, and change the car."

Sometimes it's hard to know what to keep and what to throw away! Often we hold on to feelings and fears that should be discarded.

If the memory of a real or imagined hurt is holding you back from making the best of your life, throw it away. Forgive the person who hurt you. As long as you cling to the memory, you can't go forward. Like a stalled car, you are stuck. In fact, you are a prisoner. But if you forgive the person who hurt you, you can get past the hurt and move forward with your life.

O God of all goodness and grace, fill my heart with love. Help me to forgive others as you forgive me.

Two small boys were walking in the state capitol and noticed a huge, abstract painting. One looked at the other and said, "Let's get out of here before someone thinks we did it!"

Like those two boys, we often live with guilt—sometimes earned and sometimes not. Although a legitimate guilty conscience can lead us to repentance, an undeserved guilty conscience is not a healthy motivator for living the Christian life. We are called to serve God out of love, not fear or guilt. How wonderful it is to be free of the chains of unnecessary guilt!

Help me to let go of the unnecessary guilt in my life, Lord, and to seek your forgiveness for the wrong that I commit.

Kids today have become very sophisticated. A child told a neighbor friend, "Let's play doctor. You operate, and I'll sue."

Have you ever ignored the gospel lesson when you air your grievances with anyone who has abused or harmed you? Have you ever failed to give someone an opportunity to solve problems with you before going to court? What would be your counsel to a child who thinks that suing is the first step in settling disagreements?

Dear Father, I hate problems. Please help me to grow through them instead of avoiding them. And please help me to settle all differences by remembering to use your gifts of love and respect for others.

A traffic officer was checking the license of the driver he had stopped. "You're supposed to be wearing glasses," he said to the driver.

"But officer," the driver replied, "I have contacts."

"I don't care who you know," the officer snarled. "You're violating the law."

As people of faith, we have a relationship with God through Christ which grants us certain "privileges," but not for our own personal gain or advantage over others. In the life of faith it is indeed "Who you know," but we also must ask, "What would You have me to do?"

O God, may I never use you for personal gain.

I had taken on the job of babysitting my granddaughter while her parents took a trip. By the third day, she started misbehaving. When I chided her, she replied, "If I waste my good manners every day, I won't have any left when company comes."

Do we save our "good manners" for outsiders and forget to lavish them on our nearest and dearest? God knows our lives are filled with stress and wants us to lean on him and trust him to ease our burdens. By drawing on God's love, we can be more loving to others.

Gracious God, help me to reflect your love to all I meet today.

A sign over a row of hooks in an office read, "For supervisory personnel only." Someone had written below it, "May also be used for coats and hats."

We live in a world that places great importance on one's status, rights, and privileges, yet these things have no significance in the kingdom of God. God calls each of us to be a servant—regardless of age, race, gender, education, position, income, or any other worldly measure. When we follow Christ's example, putting others' needs before our own, we are freed from the destructiveness of our own self-importance.

Help me, Lord, to put on humility and meekness so that I may serve others with a sincere heart.

A young man finished his tour of duty, was released from the Air Force, and enrolled in a local college. A few days into his first term, he was late to class.

The professor angrily asked him, "When you were late in the service, what did they say to you?"

"When I came in late," the student replied, "they stood up, saluted, and said, 'How are you this morning, Colonel, Sir?'"

Positions of power and rank in society may change as we move in and out of different communities and institutions. But in the kingdom of God, such concerns as social status and individual achievement are replaced by the sharing of talents and gifts for the good of the fellowship and the carrying out of the Great Commission. We all become as "one in the Spirit."

O God, who calls us to be the Body of Christ, remind me to whom I give my time, my talents, my gifts, and my presence.

Two women spent all afternoon quoting Bible verses to each other, each woman trying to prove she was the better Christian. When one of them finally left, the hostess remarked to her husband, "She is a good Christian, but I do believe I live closer to the Lord."

Her husband thought it over and replied, "Neither of you is crowding him any."

Like these two women, the disciples also argued with one another about who was the greatest. Jesus said to them, "Whoever wants to be first must be last of all and servant of all" (Mark 9:35b). The greatest in the kingdom of heaven, he said, is the one who becomes humble like a child (Matt. 18:4). We are not to call attention to our "righteousness," as the Pharisees did, but to live as humble servants.

Help me, Lord, to become humble like a child.

91

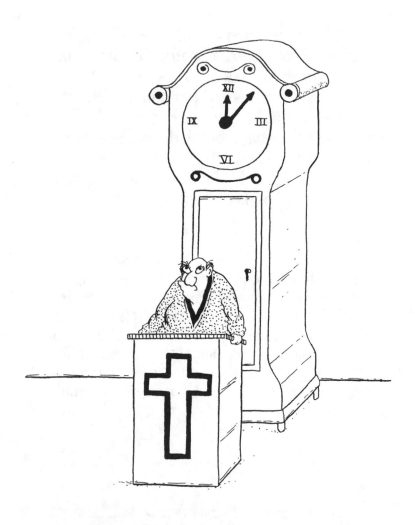

The pastor of a church announced that if the congregation reached their fund-raising goal, he would allow a clock to be installed beside the pulpit. If they exceeded the goal by $2,000, he would allow it to be plugged in. If the donation exceeded the goal by $5,000, he promised to look at the clock!

All of us have something that motivates us. This pastor believes getting out of church on time will motivate people to give. For others, giving is motivated by attaining the goal of heaven. But the best motivation of all is giving for the benefit of another; "for God so loved the world that he gave his only begotten son . . ."

Gracious Father, thank you for your magnificent gift. I pray that Jesus will be my motivation and inspiration to give often and always for the sake of others.

A neatly printed message was taped to a vending machine. It read: "This machine reserves the right to refuse service to anyone, anytime."

At one time or another, we all have been frustrated by a vending machine "on strike." We smile knowingly at the idea of a vending machine's conscious refusal of service. Yet how often have we had similar attitudes toward others who need our assistance?

Jesus taught that we are to love our neighbors as ourselves. And when asked, "Who is my neighbor?" his answer was, essentially, anyone who is in need. As Jesus demonstrated by his own example, no one is to be excluded. We are to be a servant to all.

Dear God, give me the attitude of a willing servant, and help me to see everyone as my neighbor.

McPherson

A man, with toolbox in hand, rang the doorbell. When a woman opened the door, he said, "I'm the plumber. You called for me."

The woman looked puzzled. "No, I didn't," she said.

He referred to his paperwork. "Aren't you Mrs. Johnson?"

"No, she moved away six months ago," the woman answered.

"How do you like that!" the man cried. "They call for a plumber and say it's an emergency, and then they move!"

God "calls" us in many ways and many voices. Sometimes we feel compelled to reach out to someone or lend a helping hand. Other times we are invited to give of our time or talents. Still other times an opportunity simply presents itself. How do we respond? Do we take action quickly and eagerly or procrastinate and make excuses? Are we sensitive to God's call or do we ignore or question it?

Listen for God's call today.

Dear God, help me to hear and respond to your call.

The fourth-grade teacher said to her class, "Now students, we're going to study the Arctic regions and the Eskimos. I'm sure you have all studied your lessons. Rob, what do you know about the Eskimos?"

Rob, who hadn't studied his lesson, answered, "They are famous for their delicious pies!"

Jesus' parable of the ten virgins, recounted in Matthew's Gospel, reminds us that we must always be prepared for anything God might ask of us. Part of being prepared involves planning ahead; part of being prepared involves a willingness to be open to challenge and change.

Dear God, help me be ready to accept whatever you might ask me to do.

A Sunday school teacher asked the children just before she dismissed them to go to church, "And why is it necessary to be quiet in church?"

Annie replied, "Because people are sleeping."

Unfortunately, Annie's observation is often true! Although our eyes may be open during worship, many of us are asleep mentally and spiritually. We need to be awakened to God's transforming power. Only when we are truly awake, experiencing and reaffirming our love for God and one another, are we empowered for the challenge of daily living.

Open my eyes, that I may see, all of the love Thou hast for me. Open my eyes, illumine me, Spirit divine.

A father told his young son that he wanted to tell him the facts of life. He was stumped by the boy's first question: "How many are there?"

On certain days we're all a bit like that young son. We'd like to have tidy answers to difficult questions; we long for simplicity and understanding and a little peace and quiet in our lives. But on most days we thrive on the complexities of God's creation and the many ways in which we are called to respond to it.

Be with me, Lord, when I am tempted to hasten past you and not stay mindful of my promises to you.

A mother asked her daughter why she put her new flashlight in the drawer with its light turned on.

She answered, "Well, Momma, that's so I can find it quickly when I need it."

Jesus is the Light of the world. Let us keep him "on" all the time so that we can find him quickly when we need him.

Dear God, thank you for sending your Son to brighten our lives and light our pathways to you.

As the crowd left the theater, two men hailed the same taxi. After arguing about it for a moment, one man graciously gave it to the other. When he returned to the curb, his wife berated him for letting the other man have the taxi. He responded, "I figured he needs it worse than we do. He's late to his karate class!"

Sometimes we do the right thing for the wrong reason. Our motives are self-serving. As the saying goes, our hearts are not in the right place.

Jesus said that the pure in heart—those whose hearts are in the right place—are blessed. When we strive to be pure in heart and to live as Jesus instructed us to live, we want to do the right thing for the right reason. We no longer serve self; we serve God. And the evidence of this is a life marked by the fruit of the Spirit: joy, peace, patience, kindness, generosity, faithfulness, gentleness, and self-control.

Help me, O God, to live a life marked by the fruit of the Spirit.

A woman called her doctor at home, and the doctor's young son answered the phone.

"Is the doctor there?" she asked.

"No, she isn't," he said.

"When will she be back?"

"I don't know," the boy replied. "There was an accident, and she's out on an eternity call."

Jesus' life was an "eternity call" to us. We answer in the way we live our lives. What is your answer?

Eternal Father, take us in your gentle arms and make our lives a reflection of your Son, Jesus Christ.

A father was chatting with his ecology-minded teenage son. "I can't stand all this trash, pollution, and dirt," the son said.

"Okay," replied the father, "let's get out of your room and talk somewhere else."

Often the concerns at hand are in the eye of the beholder! Before we set out on a mission to correct this or that, perhaps we should be sure we understand clearly the task before us—especially if we want to enlist the aid of our brothers and sisters in Christ. They just might see things a bit differently!

O God, be thou my vision!

A young woman called a newspaper and asked for the food editor. When she came on the line, the young woman said, "I'm preparing a dinner for guests. I've bought a nine-pound turkey and want to cook it in the microwave. Please tell me how long I should cook it."

"Just a minute," the editor said as she turned away to check her references, never hearing the young woman say, "Oh, thank you so much. You've been a big help!"

How often are we like this young woman in our prayer life? Conditioned by our "instant results" society, we don't want to wait for God's answer. We want it now. "Why is it taking so long for God to answer my prayer?" we wonder.

The Scriptures tell us that we are to be patient and persistent in prayer. Sometimes God answers our prayers immediately; sometimes gradually. And sometimes God's answer is "wait." Although we do not like to wait, we can be confident that, in God's time, an answer will come; and though it may not be the answer we expect, it will be the answer we need.

O God, help me to be more patient and persistent in prayer.

A candidate for political office asked a constituent what he thought of the speech he had just given on the agricultural program.

"Not bad," replied the voter, "but rain would have done more good!"

We all know people who "talk a good game" but don't play. They're all talk and no action—and sometimes "they" are us! We have the best of intentions, but . . .

To be a disciple of Christ is to be committed to action. Unless we act on our faith, our faith withers and dies. Jesus said, "Come, follow me."

I want to follow you faithfully, Lord. Transform my fear, selfishness, laziness, and uncertainty into unyielding commitment.

A little boy sent a "get well quick" card to his grandfather in the hospital. Inside the card he wrote, "Dear Grandpa, Mama tells me that you went to the hospital for some tests. I hope you get an 'A'! Love, Billy."

How often have you been worried or troubled only to be uplifted by the hopeful spirit of a child? Children look to us for guidance and direction, but often it is they who lead us. "And a little child shall lead them" (Isa. 11:6).

Dear God, I give thanks for all the children who have brightened my life.

A father was reading a story about Pooh Bear getting stuck in Rabbit's door to his four-year-old daughter. "Each day he got a little fatter," he read.

The father had read the book several times over a period of weeks and realized something was puzzling his daughter. Finally, as she peered at the pictures, she asked, "Where's the little fatter?"

If we don't get things right at the beginning, everything following will be wrong. The child's next questions would surely be, "What is a little fatter?" and "What did Pooh do with all those fatters he collected every day?" Whether we're reading Pooh stories about "getting a little fatter" or reading the Bible about "removing a plank from our eye," we need to get the basics right.

Dear God, help me to be willing to spend extra time getting the basics right before I try to get more sophisticated. Help me to keep a simple faith.

A young barber, when asked if he had anything for gray hair, responded, "Yes, sir, a lot of respect."

When you were taught to respect your elders, did you think you should respect them just because they were older than you were? At some point we learn that our elders have a great deal to teach us, not simply because they are older but because they have experienced life. We can often see in our elders wisdom, understanding, and inspiration. They are one of God's gifts to us.

Dear God, thank you for the presence of elders— the ones I know now and the ones who influenced me from my earliest days.

Three-year-old Sandy came into the living room, picked up a picture of herself from the coffee table, took a good look at it, and said, "That's the cutest thing I've ever seen!"

Little Sandy is on to something. Certainly we can become overly concerned with our physical appearance and our own self-interests, but we can also forget to love ourselves. God made us in his image. He wants us to see ourselves as his children—children with many talents that can be used to serve others.

Dear Heavenly Father, look down on your children and teach us to love ourselves and others as you love us.

A fourth-grade class had a substitute teacher one day. The teacher was doing the roll call, and when she came to the name "Jesús," a Latino name, she pronounced it Jesus, like the name of God's Son. No one answered, so she repeated it the same way. In a quiet voice, one of the students said, "He's here; he's all around us. But my mom says sometimes he takes a while to answer us."

Sometimes God answers prayer by saying, "Wait." Do you have the faith that if you wait long enough, God will answer you—perhaps not in the way you want, but in the way that is best for you? Do you have the faith to obey that answer? If we trust in God, he will never fail us.

Dear Lord, help me to be patient and trusting in prayer.

Generally speaking, men and women respond to questions and situations quite differently.

Ask a man where he got a cake, and he'll tell you, "At the grocery store." Ask a woman the same question, and she'll ask, "What's the matter with it?"

But ask a woman how she bruised her toe, and she'll say, "I kicked a chair." Ask a man the same question, and he'll reply, "Somebody left a chair in the middle of the room!"

Men and women may indeed have tendencies to respond differently in similar situations. How might this affect our life in the community of faith? Whatever our experience or our studies tell us, we are always called to seek to understand and act upon the Word, which says, "There is neither . . . male nor female, for you are all one in Christ Jesus" (Gal. 3:28 NIV).

Dear Lord, help me to focus not on differences in gender but on our oneness in you.

My grandson was turning seven the next day. I asked him how he felt about that. "Great!" he shouted. "The older you get, the better life is!"

If only we could keep that attitude! Whether we are young, middle-aged, or mature in years, God has good things in store for us. Even though sometimes it seems there is only pain and hardship in this life, there are blessings to be found all around us. Often they are "blessings in disguise." May God open our eyes and fill our hearts with gratitude.

Dear God, give me gratitude for the obvious blessings in my life, and help me to discern those blessings in disguise.

A little boy told his aunt, "I think God sends twins to families on purpose."

"And why is that?" she asked.

"Because little kids are scared to be alone."

This little boy is very much aware of the universal human need for companionship. Whether we are in the presence of family, friends, acquaintances, strangers—or solely in the presence of God—we are never really alone.

Dear Lord, help me to see you in the faces of my fellow human beings.